I AM
AND
I WILL

THE A-Z OF POSITIVE AFFIRMATIONS
AND CALL TO ACTIONS

SHERRISE 'LDN' MARSHALLECK

Shurise

Marshallen

NYC 2024

I AM AND I WILL

ISBN (978-1-09838-363-3)

Printed in the United States of America.

Cover Design by LivThoughtfully

For information address Sherrise 'LDN' Marshalleck,
P.O. Box 349 Washingtonville, NY 10992 or Info@ChattinWithLDN.com

THIS BOOK IS **DEDICATED** TO NIEL!

I AM...
YOUR **RELENTLESS** BIG SISTER

AND

I WILL...
ALWAYS **LOVE, RESPECT, PROTECT,**
AND **BE THERE** FOR YOU!

CONTENTS

HI, I'm Sherrise! When I moved to "The Big Apple" (New York City) back in 2004 people would constantly ask "where are you from?" I had (and still have) the thickest British accent, I'd reply "London" and voila my nickname was born. I wouldn't be me if I didn't remix the remix, I'd introduce myself as **LDN** (pronounced el-dee-N), which is what us Londoners call London. **#IYKYK = If you know you know!**

Let me be very clear my family and other British people refuse to call me London, the odd one or two will "put some respect" on the LDN tag! Not without asking "what's your real name?" or people stateside who are amazed that my mum would name me London, with comments such as "wait, your name is London and you're from London!" or "London from London, that's cool."

By now you know my "real" name, I wouldn't change it for the world, and in this chapter of my life (no pun intended) it is quintessential that I make it known that there is power in words (which I'll illustrate in the pages to follow) and in proving this point I'll share the definition of my name, **Sherrise**.

"When I named you I thought I was being unique and you'd be the only one with your name. I was inspired by the pronunciation of the color Cerise. I read a baby book and found a name spelt similarly to yours and the definition was **creative** and **artistic**." My mum shared with me.

I recently did my own research and here are some words that are associated with my name: **autodidact** (one of my favorite words), **charming, creative, leading an exciting and eventful life, loving, nurturer, peacemaker, promoter of new ideas, spiritually intense,** and **versatile.**

These words resonated with me and made me think about what my grandma had said to me growing up. "Sherrise when you were born, you weren't breathing. The umbilical cord strangled you, you were dead. I prayed that God would give you life because I don't know what your mother would have done if you didn't come back to us that day." Her prayer was "God, please give this little girl life and if it's in your will use her for good! Allow her to be a positive influence on those she meets!"

If it were not for those powerful words, I would doubt the strength that any could possibly have, and this book wouldn't exist. I feel that it's my moral obligation to show you the intrinsic power of words.

Here's a simple and very relevant example, at the end of 2020 I wrote the following on a piece of paper: "*I am... A WRITER & I will... PUBLISH MULTIPLE WORKS OF LITERATURE*" I placed it in a frame, hung it (at eye level) next to my bedroom door, and read it aloud daily, until it was all I could think about. If you're reading this, you're holding the power of words in your hands!

I am deeply moved that you're welcoming me into your life and adding my first piece of literature to your library!

This isn't just a book, think of it as your personal source of strength, a battery pack when your energy is low, that wise friend who is always dropping gems or cheering you on from the sidelines! *I AM AND I WILL* is filled with daily affirmations and very specific call to actions, consider it your dictionary of affirmations!

You can read this book on-the-go, when you feel inspired, reflective, or in need of some encouragement!

You know the moments when:

- Your loved ones are too busy (or otherwise engaged) and can't console you
- You aren't feeling 100% but need a little pep talk or reminder that you're **amazing**, **blessed**, **highly favored**, **loved**, and **one of a kind**
- You're about to embark on a new endeavor and need to boss up
- You dimmed your light and needed a quick reminder that "**your presence is the present**"

Or... Someone made you question yourself!

However you choose to read this book is entirely up to you! Whatever you do please enjoy and cherish it, allow it to travel with you as you learn and grow through life. May it fill you with all the inspiration you need to become the best version of yourself.

SHARING IS CARING

Pay it forward by empowering and inspiring others.

Here's how:

1. Call, text, DM, email, meet up with loved ones, or start a conversation with a new friend (some may call them a stranger)
2. Randomly open a page of this book
3. Read them an affirmation or have an *I AM AND I WILL* affirmation/reading party (p.s. make sure I get an invite)

Lastly, the next page is especially for you; to make your own affirmation! Feel free to remove the page, frame it, and place it wherever you'd like it to be seen. Maybe you'd prefer to put it in a safe(r) place or keep it where it is, that's fine too.

Once you've made your affirmation take a picture of it, tag me: **@ChattinWithLDN**, or use the **#IAAIW** hashtag, email me (if you'd like a little chat), and because I truly care please let me know what you think about the book; **LDN@ChattinWithLDN.com**.

Get your exclusive *I AM AND I WILL* merchandise via: www.SherriseMarshalleck.com.

Thank you for being you!

I AM...

- -

AND

I WILL...

- -

- -

MANIFEST IT, AFFIRM IT, BELIEVE IT, AND BECOME IT!

I AM...
ABLE

AND

I WILL...
USE MY
PHYSICAL/
MENTAL
STRENGTH TO
SUCCEED

I AM...
ACCOMPLISHED

AND

I WILL...
USE MY
EDUCATION,
SKILLS AND
TRAINING FOR
GOOD

I AM...
ACTIVE

AND

I WILL...
ENGAGE MY
PHYSICALITY

I AM...
ADAPTABLE

AND

I WILL...
ADJUST TO NEW SITUATIONS

I AM...
ADEQUATE

AND

I WILL...
BE ACCEPTED

I AM...
ADMIRED

AND

I WILL...
BE HIGHLY REGARDED

I AM...
ADORED

AND

I WILL...
BE DEEPLY LOVED AND RESPECTED

I AM...
ADVENTUROUS

AND

I WILL...
TAKE RISKS,
LEARN, AND
experience
new THINGS

I AM...
ALLURING

AND

I WILL...
FASCINATE
OTHERS

I AM...
AMAZING

AND

I WILL...
CONTINUE
TO BE
ASTONISHING

I AM...
AMBITIOUS

AND

I WILL...
SUCCEED

I AM...
APPRECIATIVE

AND

I WILL...
CHERISH WHAT I HAVE

I AM...
ATTENTIVE

AND

I WILL...
PAY CLOSE ATTENTION TO LIFE'S MANY MARVELS

I AM...
BALANCED

AND

I WILL...
REMAIN
EQUAL, FAIR, AND RELIABLE

I AM...
BEAUTIFUL

AND

I WILL...
ALLOW MY BEAUTY TO SHINE FROM WITHIN AND MAINTAIN MY excellence

I AM...
BLESSED

AND

I WILL...
REMAIN
GRATEFUL

I AM...
BLISSFUL

AND

I WILL...
ALLOW MY **JOY** AND **HAPPINESS** TO OVERFLOW

I AM...
BOLD

AND

I WILL...
BE CONFIDENT
AND
COURAGEOUS

I AM...
BRAVE

AND

I WILL...
BE FEARLESS

I AM...
CALM

AND

I WILL...
REMAIN PEACEFUL AND NOT SUCCUMB TO ANGER, ANXIETY, OR DOUBT

SHERRISE MARSHALLECK

I AM...
CAPABLE

AND

I WILL...
BE
COMPETENT
AND EFFICIENT

I AM...
CARING

AND

I WILL...
BE KIND, SHOW CARE, AND CONCERN FOR OTHERS

SHERRISE MARSHALLECK

I AM...
CERTAIN

AND

I WILL...
LEAD WITH SURETY AND CONVICTION

I AM...
COGNIZANT

AND

I WILL...
Be **AWARe**

SHERRISE MARSHALLECK

I AM...
COMMITTED

AND

I WILL...
WHOLEHEARTEDLY SHOWCASE MY
DEDICATION

I AM...
COMMUNICATIVE

AND

I WILL...
COMMUNICATE
EFFECTIVELY

I AM...
COMPASSIONATE

AND

I WILL...
SHOW SYMPATHY AND CONCERN FOR OTHERS

I AM...
COMPETENT

AND

I WILL...
USE MY **ABILITY,** **KNOWLEDGE,** AND *SKILLS* TO BE(COME) *SUCCESSFUL*

I AM...
CONFIDENT

AND

I WILL...
BE ASSERTIVE AND SELF-ASSURED

I AM...
CONSCIENTIOUS

AND

I WILL...
REMAIN
VIGILANT AND
ACUTELY **AWARE**

I AM...
CONSIDERATE

AND

I WILL...
BE OF
CONVENIENCE
TO OTHERS

I AM...
CONTENT

AND

I WILL...
BE PEACEFULLY HAPPY AND GRATEFUL

I AM...
COURAGEOUS

AND

I WILL...
BE **STRONG** IN THE FACE OF GRIEF OR PAIN

I AM...
CREATIVE

AND

I WILL...
use MY
IMAGINATION

SHERRISE MARSHALLECK

I AM...
DARING

AND

I WILL...
DARE TO BE
DIFFERENT AND
BOLD

I AM...

DECISIVE

AND

I WILL...

BE **FIRM** IN MY DECISION- MAKING

I AM...
DEDICATED

AND

I WILL...
BE DEVOTED TO MY PURPOSE

I AM...
DELIGHTED

AND

I WILL...
BE GLAD

I AM...
DETERMINED

AND

I WILL...
AFFIRM MY
DECISIONS

I AM...
DIVINE

AND

I WILL...
THRIVE IN MY
excellence

SHERRISE MARSHALLECK

I AM...

DRIVEN

AND

I WILL...

BE **RELENTLESS** AND **COMPELLED** TO ACCOMPLISH MY GOAL(S)

I AM...
EFFERVESCENT

AND

I WILL...
LIVE MY LIFE
ENTHUSIASTICALLY

I AM...
EFFICIENT

AND

I WILL...
BE PRODUCTIVE
AND
COMPETENT

I AM...

EMOTIONALLY-INTELLIGENT

AND

I WILL...

EXPRESS MY EMOTIONS AND BE EMPATHETIC TOWARDS OTHERS

SHERRISE MARSHALLECK

I AM...
EMPATHETIC

AND

I WILL...
UNDERSTAND THE FEELINGS OF OTHERS

I AM...
EMPOWERED

AND

I WILL...
BE
POWERFULLY
BOLD AND
TAKE CONTROL
OF MY LIFE

SHERRISE MARSHALLECK

I AM...
ENCOURAGING

AND

I WILL...
BE **POSITIVE** AND A **GREAT** **SUPPORT** TO OTHERS

I AM...
ENDEARING

AND

I WILL...
INSPIRE LOVE
AND AFFECTION

I AM...
ENERGETIC

AND

I WILL...
BE **ACTIVE** MENTALLY, PHYSICALLY, AND SPIRITUALLY

I AM...
ENGAGING

AND

I WILL...
GAIN THE
INTEREST OF
OTHERS

I AM...
ENTHUSIASTIC

AND

I WILL...
INVEST MY TIME IN WHAT TRULY INTERESTS ME

I AM...
ESSENTIAL

AND

I WILL...
ALWAYS BE OF
extreme
IMPORTANCE

SHERRISE MARSHALLECK

I AM...
ETHICAL

AND

I WILL...
BE MORALLY-SOUND

I AM...

EVEN-KEELED

AND

I WILL...

SHOWCASE
STABLE AND
CONSISTENT
CHARACTERISTICS

SHERRISE MARSHALLECK

I AM...
EVER-
CHANGING

AND

I WILL...
COMMIT
MYSELF TO
PERSONAL-
DEVELOPMENT

I AM...
EVOLVING

AND

I WILL...
CONSTANTLY
GROW,
DEVELOP, AND
FLOURISH

SHERRISE MARSHALLECK

I AM...
EXCEPTIONAL

AND

I WILL...
VALUE MY GREATNESS, INTELLIGENCE, SKILLS, AND WISDOM

I AM...

EXTRAORDINARY

AND

I WILL...

REMAIN
REMARKABLE

SHERRISE MARSHALLECK

I AM...
FAIR

AND

I WILL...
BE GENTLE, NON-VIOLENT, AND JUST

I AM...
FAITHFUL

AND

I WILL...
REMAIN **LOYAL,** **RELIABLE,** AND **UNWAVERING**

I AM...
FEARLESS

AND

I WILL...
LIVE WITHOUT FEAR

I AM...
FLEXIBLE

AND

I WILL...
BEND WITHOUT BREAKING

I AM...
FORGIVING

AND

I WILL...
NOT BE ANGRY OR RESENTFUL TOWARDS OTHERS

I AM...
FORTUNATE

AND

I WILL...
NOT TAKE MY BLESSINGS FOR GRANTED

I AM...
GENEROUS

AND

I WILL...
GIVE MORE OF MYSELF TO THE WORLD

I AM...
GENUINE

AND

I WILL...
PRESERVE MY AUTHENTICITY

SHERRISE MARSHALLECK

I AM...
GIVING

AND

I WILL...
PROVIDE CARE, LOVE, AND EMOTIONAL SUPPORT

I AM...
GLEEFUL

AND

I WILL...
FEEL AND EXPRESS MY HAPPINESS

I AM...
GRACEFUL

AND

I WILL...
BE PLEASANT
AND POLITE

I AM...
GRACIOUS

AND

I WILL...
BE **CHEERFUL,**
COURTEOUS,
AND **KIND**

I AM...
GRATEFUL

AND

I WILL...
BE
APPRECIATIVE
AND **THANKFUL**

I AM...
GREAT

AND

I WILL...

MAGNIFY MY GREATNESS

SHERRISE MARSHALLECK

I AM...
GROWING

AND

I WILL...
PROGRESS AND BECOME GREATER

I AM...
HAPPY

AND

I WILL...

BE **FILLED WITH ENJOYMENT** AND **CONTENTMENT**

I AM...
HARD-WORKING

AND

I WILL...
ALWAYS BE COMMITTED TO MY ENDEAVORS AND MAKE A TRUE EFFORT

I AM...

HARMONIOUS

AND

I WILL...

NOT BE

DISAGREEABLE
OR CREATE
DISCORD

SHERRISE MARSHALLECK

I AM...
HEALING

AND

I WILL...
ALLOW MYSELF THE **TIME** AND **SPACE** NEEDED TO HEAL

I AM...
HEALTHY

AND

I WILL...
REMAIN IN
GOOD HEALTH

SHERRISE MARSHALLECK

I AM...
HOLISTIC

AND

I WILL...
HONOR MY ENTIRE BEING (MIND, BODY, AND SOUL)

I AM...
HONEST

AND

I WILL...
TELL THE TRUTH AND BE FREE OF DECEIT

I AM...
HONORABLE

AND

I WILL...
BE HONEST
AND FAIR

I AM...
HOPEFUL

AND

I WILL...
REMAIN
OPTIMISTIC

SHERRISE MARSHALLECK

I AM...
HUMBLE

AND

I WILL...
BE MODEST

I AM...
IDEALISTIC

AND

I WILL...
WORK TOWARDS ACHIEVING UNIMAGINABLE THINGS

SHERRISE MARSHALLECK

I AM...
ILLUMINATING

AND

I WILL...
ALWAYS SHINE
(MY LIGHT)
BRIGHT

I AM...
IMPORTANT

AND

I WILL...
UPHOLD MY
VALUE/WORTH

I AM...
INCLUSIVE

AND

I WILL...
BE **UNBIASED** AND **NON-JUDGMENTAL**

I AM...

INCOMPARABLE

AND

I WILL...

NOT COMPARE MYSELF TO OTHERS

I AM...
INDEPENDENT

AND

I WILL...
BE SELF-GOVERNED AND NOT DEPEND ON OTHERS

I AM...
INFLUENTIAL

AND

I WILL...
VALUE MY INFLUENCE AND USE IT FOR GOOD

SHERRISE MARSHALLECK

I AM...
INNOVATIVE

AND

I WILL...
CREATE, INTRODUCE, AND THINK ABOUT NEW IDEAS THAT WILL POSITIVELY IMPACT OTHERS

I AM...
INQUISITIVE

AND

I WILL...
EXPLORE
THINGS THAT
AROUSE MY
CURIOSITY

I AM...
INSPIRING

AND

I WILL...
CONTINUE TO
INSPIRE OTHERS

I AM...
INSTINCTIVE

AND

I WILL...
ALLOW MY
NATURAL
ABILITIES TO
DICTATE MY
ACTIONS

SHERRISE MARSHALLECK

I AM...
INTELLECTUAL

AND

I WILL...
CONTINUE TO
NURTURE MY
INTELLECT

I AM...
INTENTIONAL

AND

I WILL...
LEAD WITH PURPOSE

I AM...
INTUITIVE

AND

I WILL...
BE STILL AND ALLOW MY MIND TO GUIDE ME

I AM...
JOVIAL

AND

I WILL...
BE CHEERFUL
AND FRIENDLY

I AM...
JOYFUL

AND

I WILL...
FEEL AND EXPRESS MY HAPPINESS

I AM...
JOYOUS

AND

I WILL...
BE FULL OF JOY

I AM...
JUBILANT

AND

I WILL...
SHOWCASE MY HAPPINESS (ESPECIALLY WHEN I SUCCEED)

I AM...
KEEN

AND

I WILL...
BE EAGER, ENTHUSIASTIC, AND SHOW INTEREST

I AM...
KIND

AND

I WILL...
Be CONSIDERATE, FRIENDLY, AND GENEROUS

I AM...
KNOWLEDGABLE

AND

I WILL...
ENHANCE MY INTELLIGENCE AND REMAIN WELL INFORMED

SHERRISE MARSHALLECK

I AM...
LIKABLE

AND

I WILL...
BE PLEASANT, FRIENDLY, AND EASY TO LIKE

I AM...
LIMITLESS

AND

I WILL...
NOT LIMIT
MYSELF

SHERRISE MARSHALLECK

I AM...
LOGICAL

AND

I WILL...
OPERATE FROM A PLACE OF **CLARITY, UNDERSTANDING,** AND ***SENSIBILITY***

I AM...
LOVING

AND

I WILL...
SHOW LOVE AND GREAT CARE FOR OTHERS

SHERRISE MARSHALLECK

I AM...
LOYAL

AND

I WILL...
ENCOURAGE, HELP, AND SUPPORT MY LOVED ONES

I AM...
LUMINOUS

AND

I WILL...
BE OF **LIGHT**
AND **POSITIVITY**

I AM...
MASTERFUL

AND

I WILL...
RELY ON MY SKILLS AND PRODUCE GREAT WORK

I AM...
MATURE

AND

I WILL...
BASK IN MY EMOTIONAL, SPIRITUAL, AND PHYSICAL GROWTH

I AM...
MEANINGFUL

AND

I WILL...
VALUE MY
IMPORTANCE

I AM...
MEDITATIVE

AND

I WILL...
BE *STILL,*
RELAXED, AND
REFLECTIVE

SHERRISE MARSHALLECK

I AM...
MEMORABLE

AND

I WILL...
MAKE A LASTING IMPRESSION ON OTHERS

I AM...
MERCIFUL

AND

I WILL...
BE
COMPASSIONATE
AND FORGIVING

SHERRISE MARSHALLECK

I AM...
MERRY

AND

I WILL...
BE CHEERFUL
AND LIVELY

I AM...

MINDFUL

AND

I WILL...

BE CONSCIOUSLY AWARE AND PRESENT

I AM...
MODEST

AND

I WILL...
NOT BE
PRETENTIOUS OR ARROGANT

I AM...

MORALLY-SOUND

AND

I WILL...

BE HIGHLY PRINCIPLED

I AM...
MOTIVATED

AND

I WILL...
ACHIEVE WHAT I SET OUT TO COMPLETE

I AM...
MULTIFACETED

AND

I WILL...
EXPLORE MY
INTRICACIES

I AM...
NEUTRAL

AND

I WILL...
BE UNBIASED
AND FAIR

I AM...
NICE

AND

I WILL...
BE CONSIDERATE, FRIENDLY, AND AGREEABLE

SHERRISE MARSHALLECK

I AM...
NON-CONFRONTATIONAL

AND

I WILL...
REMAIN CALM AND DEAL WITH OTHERS IN A SENSITIVE WAY

I AM...
NON-JUDGMENTAL

AND

I WILL...
NOT JUDGE OTHERS

I AM...
NON-REACTIVE

AND

I WILL...
THINK BEFORE I ACT OR SPEAK

I AM...
OPEN-MINDED

AND

I WILL...
CONSIDER NEW IDEAS WITHOUT PREJUDICE

I AM...
OPTIMISTIC

AND

I WILL...
BE HOPEFUL AND CONFIDENT (THROUGHOUT LIFE)

I AM...
OPULENT

AND

I WILL...
EXUDE
excellence
AND SHOWCASE
THE **VALUE/**
WEALTH OF MY
CHARACTER

I AM...
ORGANIC

AND

I WILL...
NOT FORCE MY DEVELOPMENT

I AM...
OTHER

AND

I WILL...
NOT CONFORM
OR BE DEFINED
BY A GROUP,
SYSTEM, OR THE
"NORM"

I AM...
PASSIONATE

AND

I WILL...
EXHIBIT MY FULL RANGE OF EMOTIONS

I AM...
PATIENT

AND

I WILL...
ACCEPT THAT
NOTHING
HAPPENS
BEFORE IT'S
TIME

I AM...
PEACEFUL

AND

I WILL...
FREE MYSELF
OF WHAT
DISTURBS ME
AND DOES NOT
BRING ME
TRANQUILITY

I AM...
PERSISTENT

AND

I WILL...
NOT GIVE UP

SHERRISE MARSHALLECK

I AM...
PHENOMENAL

AND

I WILL...
BE REMARKABLY EXTRAORDINARY

I AM...
PLAYFUL

AND

I WILL...
BE **CAREFREE,**
CHEERFUL,
AND **FUN**

I AM...
PLEASANT

AND

I WILL...
SHOW CARE, BE FRIENDLY, AND LIKABLE

I AM...
POISED

AND

I WILL...
BE SELF-ASSURED WITH GRACE AND ELEGANCE

SHERRISE MARSHALLECK

I AM...
POLITE

AND

I WILL...
BE RESPECTFUL
AND
CONSIDERATE

I AM...
POSITIVE

AND

I WILL...
MAKE A
POSITIVE
IMPACT ON THE
LIVES OF OTHERS

SHERRISE MARSHALLECK

I AM...
PRAYERFUL

AND

I WILL...
PRAY WITHOUT CEASING

I AM...
PRESENT

AND

I WILL...
FOCUS ON
WHAT I'M
EXPERIENCING
(IN THE CURRENT
MOMENT)

I AM...
PRINCIPLED

AND

I WILL...
BE **GUIDED** BY MY **MORALS** AND **PRINCIPLES**

I AM...
PRIVILEGED

AND

I WILL...
NOT ABUSE MY ADVANTAGES, IMMUNITIES, OR RIGHTS (OTHERWISE KNOWN AS MY PRIVILEGE)

SHERRISE MARSHALLECK

I AM...
PROACTIVE

AND

I WILL...
TAKE CONTROL
OF MY LIFE

I AM...
PRODUCTIVE

AND

I WILL...
ACHIEVE
GOOD RESULTS

SHERRISE MARSHALLECK

I AM...
PROGRESSING

AND

I WILL...
MOVE IN THE **RIGHT** **DIRECTION** (AS I PROGRESS)

I AM...
PROTECTED

AND

I WILL...
LIBERATE MYSELF FROM DANGER OR HARM

I AM...
PROUD

AND

I WILL...
HAVE RESPECT
FOR MYSELF

I AM...
QUALITATIVE

AND

I WILL...
BE **excellent**
AND OF **HIGH**
QUALITY

I AM...
RATIONAL

AND

I WILL...
THINK CLEARLY, LOGICALLY, AND SENSIBLY

I AM...

REAL

AND

I WILL...

BE **AUTHENTIC**
AND **VOID OF**
FALSITIES

I AM...
REASONABLE

AND

I WILL...
BE FAIR

I AM...
RELATABLE

AND

I WILL...
CONTINUE
BEING
TRANSPARENT
TO FORM
AUTHENTIC
CONNECTIONS

SHERRISE MARSHALLECK

I AM...
RELIABLE

AND

I WILL...
BE
TRUSTWORTHY

I AM...
REPUTABLE

AND

I WILL...
MAINTAIN A
GOOD
REPUTATION

I AM...
RESPECTED

AND

I WILL...
BE **ADMIRED** BY OTHERS FOR MY **CHARACTER,** **STRENGTH,** AND **UNIQUE QUALITIES**

I AM...
RESPECTFUL

AND

I WILL...
SHOW OTHERS
RESPECT

SHERRISE MARSHALLECK

I AM...
RESPONSIBLE

AND

I WILL...
HAVE **GOOD** **JUDGEMENT** AND THE **ABILITY TO ACT** **CORRECTLY**

I AM...
REVITALIZED

AND

I WILL...
PUT NEW LIFE AND ENERGY INTO THE WORLD

SHERRISE MARSHALLECK

I AM...
REVOLUTIONARY

AND

I WILL...
CULTIVATE NEW IDEAS WHICH WILL CREATE GREAT CHANGE

I AM...
ROBUST

AND

I WILL...
NOT COMPROMISE
MY HEALTH OR
STRENGTH

SHERRISE MARSHALLECK

I AM...
SECURE

AND

I WILL...
FEEL CONFIDENT AND FREE FROM ANXIETY OR FEAR

I AM...
SELF-ADVOCATED

AND

I WILL...
REPRESENT AND STAND UP FOR MYSELF

I AM...
SELF-AWARE

AND

I WILL...
COMMIT TO **KNOWING** AND **UNDERSTANDING MYSELF** EXCEPTIONALLY WELL

I AM...
SELF-REFLECTIVE

AND

I WILL...
EVALUATE MY OWN BEHAVIOR, EMOTIONS, FEELINGS, AND THOUGHTS

SHERRISE MARSHALLECK

I AM...
SELF-RELIANT

AND

I WILL...
RELY ON MY OWN RESOURCES

I AM...
SELFLESS

AND

I WILL...
CARE ABOUT THE NEEDS OF OTHERS

I AM...
SENSIBLE

AND

I WILL...
NOTICE AND
APPRECIATE
OTHERS

I AM...
SENSITIVE

AND

I WILL...
HAVE A
DELICATE
APPRECIATION
FOR THE
FEELINGS OF
OTHERS

I AM...
SINCERE

AND

I WILL...
SAY WHAT I GENUINELY FEEL OR BELIEVE

I AM...
SMART

AND

I WILL...
CONTINUE TO SHARPEN MY INTELLIGENCE

SHERRISE MARSHALLECK

I AM...

SOLUTION-ORIENTED

AND

I WILL...

SOLVE PROBLEMS

I AM...
SPECIAL

AND

I WILL...
BE GREAT AND exclusively Me

SHERRISE MARSHALLECK

I AM...
SPIRITUAL

AND

I WILL...
BE GUIDED BY
MY HIGHER
SELF

I AM...
STRONG

AND

I WILL...
BE POWERFUL, SELF-CONTROLLED, AND OF GOOD JUDGEMENT

SHERRISE MARSHALLECK

I AM...
SYMPATHETIC

AND

I WILL...
SUPPORT THOSE WHO ARE LESS FORTUNATE

I AM...
TEACHABLE

AND

I WILL...
LEARN FROM OTHERS AND BE RECEPTIVE TO NEW LESSONS

I AM...
TENDER

AND

I WILL...
ALLOW MYSELF
THE OPPORTUNITY
TO BE
GENTLE AND
VULNERABLE

I AM...

THANKFUL

AND

I WILL...

EXPRESS
GRATITUDE

I AM...

THOROUGH

AND

I WILL...

BE **CAREFUL,** **DETAIL-** **ORIENTED,** AND **NON-PARTIAL**

I AM...

TRANSPARENT

AND

I WILL...

SHARE MY
STORY/
TESTIMONIES

I AM...
TRUSTWORTHY

AND

I WILL...
ALWAYS BE
HONEST AND
TRUTHFUL

I AM...
TRUTHFUL

AND

I WILL...
EXPRESS THE TRUTH
(ESPECIALLY MY OWN)

SHERRISE MARSHALLECK

I AM...
TRYING

AND

I WILL...
DO MY BEST

I AM...
UNIQUE

AND

I WILL...
BE UNLIKE ANYONE else (ONE OF ONE)

I AM...
UNMATCHED

AND

I WILL...
NOT COMPETE
WITH OTHERS

I AM...
UNWAVERING

AND

I WILL...
REMAIN TRUE
TO WHO I AM
AND **STAND FIRM**
IN MY BELIEFS

I AM...
UPRIGHT

AND

I WILL...
BEHAVE
HONESTLY AND
HONORABLY

I AM...
VALUABLE

AND

I WILL...
BE USEFUL AND OF GREAT WORTH

I AM...
VERSATILE

AND

I WILL...
ADAPT

I AM...
VIGILANT

AND

I WILL...
PAY
ATTENTION,
PROCEED WITH
CAUTION, AND
AVOID DANGER

SHERRISE MARSHALLECK

I AM...
VIRTUOUS

AND

I WILL...
HAVE **HIGH** MORAL **STANDARDS**

I AM...
VIVACIOUS

AND

I WILL...
LIVE MY LIFE IN AN **ANIMATED** AND **LIVELY** WAY

I AM...
VOCAL

AND

I WILL...
USE MY VOICE TO express MY THOUGHTS, FEELINGS, AND OPINIONS

I AM...
WELL-
BALANCED

AND

I WILL...
LIVE AN
EMOTIONALLY
STABLE LIFE

I AM...
WELL-MANNERED

AND

I WILL...
BE **POLITE,** **RESPECTFUL,** AND CONSIDERATE

I AM...
WELL-RESPECTED

AND

I WILL...
BE HIGHLY REGARDED AND ADMIRED

I AM...
WELL-ROUNDED

AND

I WILL...
FULLY DEVELOP MY CHARACTER AND REMAIN BALANCED

I AM...
WHOLESOME

AND

I WILL...
NURTURE MY MENTAL, PHYSICAL, AND SPIRITUAL WELL-BEING

I AM...
WISE

AND

I WILL...
ENHANCE MY KNOWLEDGE, EXPERIENCE, AND HAVE GOOD JUDGEMENT

I AM...
WORLDLY

AND

I WILL...
REVEL IN MY WISDOM AND SOPHISTICATION

SHERRISE MARSHALLECK

I AM...
X

AND

I WILL...
REVEAL MY TRUE VALUE IN TIME

I AM...
YOUTHFUL

AND

I WILL...
BE **ENTHUSIASTIC**
AND **OPTIMISTIC**

SHERRISE MARSHALLECK

I AM...
ZEALOUS

AND

I WILL...
EXHIBIT GREAT ENERGY AND ENTHUSIASM

I AM...
ZESTFUL

AND

I WILL...
LIVE MY LIFE
EXCITEDLY

I AM...
A BOSS

AND

I WILL...
TAKE CHARGE
OF MY LIFE
AND BE
OUTSTANDING

I AM...

A CREATIVE

AND

I WILL...

BRING
UNIMAGINABLE
THINGS TO LIFE

I AM...
A GENIUS

AND

I WILL...
CHANNEL MY CLEVERNESS AND INGENUITY

I AM...
A MENTOR

AND

I WILL...
USE MY EXPERIENCE TO EMPOWER, INSPIRE, AND TRAIN OTHERS

SHERRISE MARSHALLECK

I AM...
A NURTURER

AND

I WILL...
CARE FOR AND ENCOURAGE THE GROWTH/ DEVELOPMENT OF OTHERS

I AM...
A PRIORITY

AND

I WILL...
NEVER BE OR FEEL INFERIOR

I AM...
A PROPHET/ PROPHETESS

AND

I WILL...
ADVOCATE FOR OTHERS AND BE A VISIONARY FOR NEW BELIEFS

I AM...
A STUDENT OF LIFE

AND

I WILL...
FIND VALUE
IN THE
UNEXPECTED
LESSONS LIFE
PRESENTS

I AM...
A SURVIVOR

AND

I WILL...
TRIUMPH THROUGH LIFE'S DIFFICULTIES

I AM...
A TEAM PLAYER

AND

I WILL...
CONTRIBUTE TO THE WORLD SELFLESSLY

SHERRISE MARSHALLECK

I AM...
A VESSEL

AND

I WILL...
USE MY **SKILLS**, **SPIRITUAL GIFTS**, AND **TALENTS** TO **POSITIVELY IMPACT** THE LIVES OF OTHERS

I AM...
A VISIONARY

AND

I WILL...
EFFECTIVELY PLAN FOR A BETTER FUTURE

SHERRISE MARSHALLECK

I AM...
ALL ABOUT UNITY

AND

I WILL...
UNITE WITH OTHERS TO IMPROVE THE WORLD

I AM...
AN ACTIVIST

AND

I WILL...
BRING ABOUT CHANGE

SHERRISE MARSHALLECK

I AM...
AN EXPERT

AND

I WILL...
EMBRACE MY expertise/ KNOWLEDGE

I AM...
AN INNOVATOR

AND

I WILL...
INTRODUCE OTHERS TO NEW CONCEPTS, IDEAS, AND METHODS

SHERRISE MARSHALLECK

I AM...
ANTI-RACIST

AND

I WILL...
PROMOTE RACIAL EQUALITY AND OPPOSE RACISM

I AM...
AUTHENTICALLY, ME

AND

I WILL...
CELEBRATE MY UNIQUENESS

I AM...
BREAKING CYCLES

AND

I WILL...
END BEHAVIORS AND PATTERNS WHICH DO NOT BEST SERVE ME

I AM...
CHANGING FOR THE BETTER

AND

I WILL...
CONTINUE TO evolve

SHERRISE MARSHALLECK

I AM...
DOING MY BEST

AND

I WILL...
OFFER THE HIGHEST QUALITY IN ALL THAT I DO

I AM...
FASCINATED BY MY LIFE

AND

I WILL...
ALLOW MY LIFE TO ALWAYS FASCINATE ME

SHERRISE MARSHALLECK

I AM...
FILLED WITH LOVE

AND

I WILL...
AMPLIFY AND exude LOVE

I AM...
IN CONTROL

AND

I WILL...
CREATE MY OWN NARRATIVES

I AM...
INSPIRED BY MYSELF

AND

I WILL...
BE SELF-MOTIVATED

I AM...
NOT A FOLLOWER

AND

I WILL...
LEAD MY LIFE AND ENCOURAGE OTHERS TO DO THE SAME

SHERRISE MARSHALLECK

I AM...
NOT A VICTIM

AND

I WILL...
NOT ALLOW TRAUMA TO DEFEAT OR OVERCOME ME

I AM...
NOT EASILY LED

AND

I WILL...
NOT BE LED
ASTRAY

I AM...
NOT
SUBSCRIBING TO
GENERATIONAL
CURSES

AND

I WILL...
BREAK CYCLES

I AM...
NOT VOID OF MISTAKES

AND

I WILL...
IDENTIFY MY FLAWS AND ADDRESS THEM

I AM...

OF GOOD CHARACTER

AND

I WILL...

BE WELL-INTENTIONED

I AM...
OF HIGH STANDARDS

AND

I WILL...
NOT LOWER MY STANDARDS

I AM...
PERFECTLY, IMPERFECT

AND

I WILL...
REVEL IN MY IMPERFECTIONS

I AM...

SENSITIVE TO THE NEEDS OF OTHERS

AND

I WILL...

SERVE THE WORLD

I AM...
THE BEST VERSION OF MYSELF

AND

I WILL...
BE THE BEST PERSON THAT I CAN BE

I AM...
TRYING MY BEST

AND

I WILL...
NEVER GIVE UP even WHEN THE GOING GETS TOUGH

SHERRISE MARSHALLECK

I AM...
WELCOMING PEACE INTO MY LIFE

AND

I WILL...
SAY "GOODBYE" TO WHAT DOESN'T BEST SERVE ME

I AM...
WILLING TO CHALLENGE MYSELF

AND

I WILL...
TEST MY ABILITIES

SHERRISE MARSHALLECK

I AM...
WILLING TO LEARN

AND

I WILL...
NOT SUCCUMB TO IGNORANCE
AND ACTIVELY LEARN NEW THINGS

I AM...

ABLE, ACCOMPLISHED, ACTIVE, ADAPTABLE, **ADEQUATE**, ADMIRED, **ADORED**, ADVENTUROUS, ALLURING, **AMAZING**, AMBITIOUS, **APPRECIATIVE**, ATTENTIVE, BALANCED, **BEAUTIFUL**, **BLESSED**, BLISSFUL, **BOLD**, **BRAVE**, CALM, CAPABLE, **CARING**, CERTAIN, COGNIZANT, **COMMITTED**, COMMUNICATIVE, **COMPASSIONATE**, COMPETENT, **CONFIDENT**, CONSCIENTIOUS, **CONSIDERATE**, CONTENT, **COURAGEOUS**, CREATIVE, DARING, DECISIVE, DEDICATED, DELIGHTED, **DETERMINED**, DIVINE, **DRIVEN**, **EFFERVESCENT**, EFFICIENT, EMOTIONALLY-INTELLIGENT, **EMPATHETIC**, **EMPOWERED**, ENCOURAGING, **ENDEARING**, ENERGETIC, **ENGAGING**, ENTHUSIASTIC, **ESSENTIAL**, ETHICAL, EVEN-KEELED, EVER-CHANGING, **EVOLVING**, **EXCEPTIONAL**, **EXTRAORDINARY**, FAIR, FAITHFUL, **FEARLESS**, FLEXIBLE, FORGIVING, **FORTUNATE**, GENEROUS, **GENUINE**, GIVING, GLEEFUL, GRACEFUL, **GRACIOUS**, GRATEFUL, **GREAT**, **GROWING**, HAPPY, HARD-WORKING, HARMONIOUS, **HEALING**, HEALTHY, HOLISTIC, **HONEST**, HONORABLE, HOPEFUL, **HUMBLE**, IDEALISTIC, ILLUMINATING, **IMPORTANT**, INCLUSIVE, **INCOMPARABLE**, **INDEPENDENT**, **INFLUENTIAL**, INNOVATIVE, INQUISITIVE, INSPIRING, INSTINCTIVE, **INTELLECTUAL**, INTENTIONAL, **INTUITIVE**, JOVIAL, JOYFUL, **JOYOUS**, JUBILANT, **KEEN**, KIND, **KNOWLEDGEABLE**, LIKABLE, **LIMITLESS**, LOGICAL, **LOVING**, LOYAL, **LUMINOUS**, MASTERFUL, MATURE, **MEANINGFUL**, MEDITATIVE, **MEMORABLE**, MERCIFUL, MERRY, **MINDFUL**, MODEST, MORALLY-SOUND, MOTIVATED, MULTIFACETED, NEUTRAL, **NICE**, NON-CONFRONTATIONAL, **NON-JUDGMENTAL**, NON-REACTIVE, **OPEN-MINDED**, **OPTIMISTIC**, OPULENT, ORGANIC, **OTHER**, PASSIONATE, PATIENT, PEACEFUL, **PERSISTENT**, **PHENOMENAL**, PLAYFUL, **PLEASANT**, POISED, POLITE, **POSITIVE**, PRAYERFUL, PRESENT, **PRINCIPLED**, PRIVILEGED, **PROACTIVE**, PRODUCTIVE, **PROGRESSING**, PROTECTED, **PROUD**, QUALITATIVE, RATIONAL, **REAL**, REASONABLE, RELATABLE, **RELIABLE**, REPUTABLE, **RESPECTED**, **RESPECTFUL**, RESPONSIBLE,

SHERRISE MARSHALLECK

REVITALIZE, **REVOLUTIONARY**, ROBUST, SECURE, **SELF-ADVOCATED**, SELF-AWARE, SELF-REFLECTIVE, **SELF-RELIANT**, SELFLESS, SENSIBLE, **SENSITIVE**, SINCERE, SMART, SOLUTION-ORIENTED, **SPECIAL**, SPIRITUAL, STRONG, **SYMPATHETIC**, TEACHABLE, **TENDER**, **THANKFUL**, THOROUGH, TRANSPARENT, TRUSTWORTHY, TRUTHFUL, TRYING, **UNIQUE**, **UNMATCHED**, UNWAVERING, UPRIGHT, **VALUABLE**, VERSATILE, VIGILANT, VIRTUOUS, **VIVACIOUS**, VOCAL, **WELL-BALANCED**, WELL-MANNERED, WELL-RESPECTED, WELL-ROUNDED, **WHOLESOME**, **WISE**, WORLDLY, **X**, YOUTHFUL, ZEALOUS, **ZESTFUL**, **A BOSS**, A CREATIVE, **A GENIUS**, A MENTOR, **A NURTURER**, **A PRIORITY**, A PROPHET/PROPHETESS, A STUDENT OF LIFE, **A SURVIVOR**, A TEAM PLAYER, **A VESSEL**, A VISIONARY, ALL ABOUT UNITY, **AN ACTIVIST**, AN EXPERT, AN INNOVATOR, **ANTI-RACIST**, **AUTHENTICALLY, ME**, **BREAKING CYCLES**, CHANGING FOR THE BETTER, **DOING MY BEST**, FASCINATED BY MY LIFE, **FILLED WITH LOVE**, IN CONTROL, **INSPIRED BY MYSELF**, NOT A FOLLOWER, **NOT A VICTIM**, NOT EASILY LED, **NOT SUBSCRIBING TO GENERATIONAL CURSES**, NOT VOID OF MISTAKES, OF GOOD CHARACTER, OF HIGH STANDARDS, **PERFECTLY, IMPERFECT**, SENSITIVE TO THE NEEDS OF OTHERS, **THE BEST PERSON THAT I CAN BE**, TRYING MY BEST, **WELCOMING PEACE INTO MY LIFE**, WILLING TO CHALLENGE MYSELF, **WILLING TO LEARN**!

AND

I WILL...

SUCCEED

"ALLOW YOUR WORDS TO EMPOWER YOU"

ACKNOWLEDGMENTS

My life wouldn't be what it is without the grace of God and I'm extremely thankful, humbled, and happy to be here on this earth. God listened to my pleading grandma as I laid lifeless at the hospital; one month premature and at a meager 5lbs 4oz. Without that miraculous testimony I wouldn't exist! The testimonies I could share are boundless so thank God for molding me into the ever-growing, ever-learning, unapologetic, spiritually intense Sherrise that I am today!

Grandma, Thank you so very much for such a specific and meaningful prayer on the day of my birth. You have always had faith in me and continue to express how proud you are of me. Thank you for being the first person I had the pleasure of meeting and someone that I still revere! Your passion, relentlessness, strength, and intuitive nature have inspired me throughout the course of my life. Ultimately rubbing off on me and has helped to shape my morals, principles, and beliefs. Thank you for always putting me in my place when I go off course and for encouraging me to write *I AM AND I WILL*.

Mum, I'd need an entire book to fully address how thankful I am for you! You have invested everything and more into your Sherrise (**TLOYL4AOYD**)! You always allowed me to explore my creativity, express myself, and not take "No" for an answer! You've always been the version of strength that's on brand! An example of excellence! As long as I live I pray that you know how very special you are to me. The love that I have for you is far from frivolous and one that I'll always pour into! The sacrifices you have made for me are countless! No one understands our journey and it'll remain ours to cherish (the highs and lows). *Sorry, I have to stop here. Please wipe your tears, better yet look over I'll hand you the tissue, and give you a big hug! Thank you for always reppin'!

Papa Ray! You're a Don! Honestly! Your mind is the sharpest, wisest, wittiest, and the only one that can nearly test mine (lol that's me being cheeky)! The other day I wrote the following down on a piece of paper "my dad is my personal journal" Do you know how thankful and honored I am to have you in my life? The humblest moment is when you called me your best friend! I will not take my position as your BFF lightly! Just know that you inspire me as much as you say I inspire you! Thank you for always being ready for our very intense and long conversations as well as challenging my every thought even when I can't get a word in edgewise.

Mama, Here's a little poem for you!

My special Grace,
No one can ever take your place.
You more than live up to your namesake,
Elegance is what you always display!

Auntie Angela, you are what millennials would call "The Rich Aunt" you introduced me to the world of luxury and I'm not just talking about fashion, although we could take it there! Thank you for also setting such a high standard, I've always looked up to you. Thinking about it now you're definitely the inspiration for my bag, trainer, and coat collection(s). You didn't have to teach me upfront lessons, I have legitimately been watching you from the sidelines all of my life taking notes. From the dinner parties to our trips to Paris and Switzerland. You introduced me to a lifestyle/world I wouldn't have otherwise been exposed to and what many other South Londoners have yet to experience. P.S. you also are living proof that no woman should ever settle! So thank you for being the subtle boss of all bosses!!!

Tasha, there is no one stronger than you, to me! Thank you for always challenging me when I was being a wimp or teasing me for "wasting" your paper when I was younger; literally drawing and writing on all the available paper in your house. Your directness allowed me to stand up to bullies at school and you inadvertently made me have thick skin when people used to call me "skinny" or "four eyes." When I'd hear people's feeble attempts to rattle my cage I'd think, "You can't test me because my aunt don't play!" Thanks also for allowing Liam to stay at our house he was my little brother way before Niel's arrival. This helped me to share and not grow up to be a spoilt brat lol.

Uncle Robert (Imagine I'm here acting like I don't just call you Robert lol) thank you for showing me what grind looks like! After grandad you are my first example of an entrepreneur. I'll always be your "spare rib" (the plant based type) thank you also for being a listening ear when I can't make sense of things and for being a solid man in my eyes!

Auntie A - Amanda (Yes, you) I always question whether we are actually sisters because we have the most unconventional auntie-niece relationship... Nonetheless I can't thank you enough for being there for me no matter what, even when I know you're otherwise engaged and could careless about what I'm talking about. You still sit there on the phone "yep" "Ummmmm" "yeah" "I get you!" Just know I know you aren't listening but care enough not to leave me in the lurch! You are the most straight talking person I know and one of a few that will call me out or tell me you don't like something; even if it won't be well received! That's exactly why I come running to you for advice because you aren't afraid to tell me the absolute truth! Although you're a toughie your heart is diamond encrusted, platinum.

Rochelle, Cuzzie! Thank you for being you! Unfiltered, thoughtful, conscientious, straight talking, unapologetic, honest, vulnerable, tough, intelligent, and so much more! You are a dynamic person who inspires my thoughts! You drop gems and leave me with them for weeks before our next conversation. You constantly explore your mental and the minds of others to answer complex equations that I enjoy working out! Thank you for being a whole person who offers your entire being to the people you love and highly regard. Most importantly thank you for welcoming me into your world and always reserving the seat next to you for me.

Oi, **Liam**! My cuz-brother! Thank you for valuing me and making me feel special without actually saying a thing or for whispering "I love you too" before we get off our hour long calls. Thank you for making me roll my eyes and laugh in the same second! You are one of the most annoyingly funny people I know! But as comical as you are you're even more conscious. The (life) chess player that people would otherwise overlook yet you'd be the reigning champ! So thanks for your subtle greatness.

Tiarna, my dearest little cousin! You don't understand how happy I was to meet you when you were born! I literally knew I had to be a great example because you gave me a reason to be socially responsible, finish college, and work hard to show you what a good example looked like. As I've evolved my version of "good example" has changed into pep talks, our empowering conversations, and sharing my mistakes. I share my testimonies/stories so you don't have to experience what I have! I'm always here for you! You're going to be such a success and I can't wait to celebrate each of your milestones! Cheers in advance.

Niel, My Baby Boo! You charge me up! You're my #1 supporter and I'm yours too! You know that your big sister will go to war for you! But please choose your battles wisely because I'm getting old... Thank you for being creative and inspiring me as you learn and grow I'm definitely learning so much from you!

Ayannah & Ariella, my darlings! Thank you for always welcoming me into your world's and amazing me as you grow up to be such lovely young ladies! I could sit on FaceTime with you both for hours and not get bored! I want you to know that when you were born your mum said "Sherrise, make sure you have an internship for the girls when they get older" and that was before I had my company! Your mummy, saw my vision and believed in me, but I want more for you! So let's make you your own businesses so that you don't have to work for anyone, including me!

Steve, Thank you for sitting through my many rants and controversial conversations which have spurred many differences in opinions. Your patience is unmatched and I truly appreciate your candor. You've also shown me what it means to be content and loyal.

Mr. E, You are one of the wisest, funniest, and most optimistic people I know! I'm humbled and beyond grateful to have you in my life and that you make me a priority in yours! It is with pleasure that I thank you for your continued support and investment in me and our unbreakable bond!

Ricky, Mi Chargie! Yuh dun kno how di ting set already! **To the rest of my enormous family** I thank you too because you've each touched my life in a special and unique way. Helping to shape me.

Olivia, Thank you for being such a lovely friend! Your conscientiousness and kind hearted nature is unmatched. The *I AM AND I WILL* cover art is a gift that I couldn't have asked anyone else to present me with. In the busiest and most hectic portion of your life you set time aside to make me a priority! I think about meeting you at the dinner event we both attended independently and I remember calling my mum that night declaring that we'd be lifelong friends; and here we are. During this very important time of my life you've been right there! Thank you so very much!

Emilia my twin flame! The day I met you was the day my life changed! You touched my heart so generously, you have been a sister to me! You feel when I feel and have been instrumental in my journey for the last few years, especially during this chapter! There have been many moments when you were busy but you made the time for a "quick" chat to get the smallest detail squared away! You know what has helped me the most? The times when sweeterman Cairo calls to speak to "Auntie Reese" or to show me he's a "big boy" the best gift you could offer me are those moments! Obrigada.

Kerry, although you're my aunt's best friend you're family to us all! I'm so grateful for your sound words of advice and wisdom! You are strong and show me that love is the answer in every situation. You have been a source of serenity during some very challenging times. Thank you for summing me up in a few paragraphs (for the bio) and making me notice my strength when I'm busy helping others and paying myself the least attention!

My **Dilly**, You are exceptional and have inspired me immensely throughout the years. Your mummy chapter is the most inspiring yet! I thank you for offering up the most encouraging words which gave me fuel for this book! I love you.

Ant, No amount of distance can affect the influence you've had on this book. We connected over music years ago, you devoted your time as an intern at Chattin' With LDN, and our bond has become stronger over time. You're one of my favorite people in this world. Thank you for being you and for bringing peace and tranquility into my life.

To my loved ones, friends, community, supporters, and those who have joined me on my journey, I thank you for "flexing with me" it's been an interesting journey; interviews, celeb events, pink lipstick, music videos, top buns, eccentric clothing, studio appearances, the random silliness I used to post on insta, and so much more memories that I'll leave in the past... Thank you for loving me enough to still be here.

For anyone that has allowed me into their lives whether for a second, minute, hour, day, week, month, year, or more you're a part of my story I wouldn't change our encounter(s) for anything!

To my new friends those who have been introduced to me for the first time! **WELCOME**, we are now mates :)

To you, the new owner of this love infused body of work! Thank you, for investing in yourself because that's what you did when you chose *I AM AND I WILL*!

I love you all <3

REFERENCES

What Does "Sherrise" Mean, Accessed April 29th 2021
through http://www.sevenreflections.com/name/sherrise/

INDEX

SHERRISE MARSHALLECK

SHERRISE MARSHALLECK

ABOUT SHERRISE

Sherrise Marshalleck, also known as **LonDoN** is an adept creative, with over 10 years of experience in Brand Partnerships, Business and Talent Management, Consultancy, Content Creation and Event Curation.

Acknowledged for her authenticity and strong dedication to improving the lives of others, Sherrise is a true maverick who disrupts spaces; creating opportunities, taking risks, and bringing the underrepresented to the forefront.

As an advocate of introspection, self-love and personal exploration she encourages open and honest conversations (especially with self). Sherrise has an aptitude for allowing people to be their truest self and has a welcoming spirit which lends to others sharing their story and a part of their lives with her!

Sherrise is highly intentional, integrity driven and fearless. Here to captivate the hearts of all she meets, with a continued focus on wellness and mindset.

Join her: www.SherriseMarshalleck.com | @ChattinWithLDN
www.ChattinWithLDN.com | LDN@ChattinWithLDN.com